As Heavy As

Lee made a ball
with some red dough.
"Look at this ball,"
she said to Sam.
"It is heavy."

Sam got a big block out of the box.

"This block will be **as heavy as** the ball,"
he said.

"No, Sam," said Lee.

"That block is too big.

It is **too heavy**."

Sam looked in the box of blocks again.

He looked for a smaller block.

"This block is smaller," he said.

"It will be **as heavy as** the ball."

"No, Sam," said Lee.

"That block is too small.

It's not **as heavy as** the ball."

"Look at this block, Lee," said Sam.

"It's not too big

and it's not too small.

This block will be **as heavy as** the ball."

"Yes!" said Lee. "Look!"

Lee got an orange from her school bag.

"Is this orange **as heavy as** the ball?"

she said.

Sam looked at the ball and the orange. "Your orange is **as heavy as** the ball," he said.

too heavy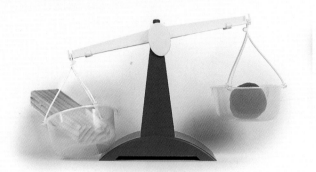

not as heavy as

as heavy as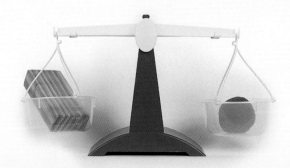